But Is It Art?

Art Installations

Alix Wood

Gareth Stevens
PUBLISHING

Please visit our website, **www.garethstevens.com**. For a free color catalog of all our high-quality books, call toll free 1-800-542-2595 or fax 1-877-542-2596

Library of Congress Cataloging-in-Publication Data

Wood, Alix.
 Art installations / Alix Wood.
     pages cm. — (But is it art?)
 Includes index.
 ISBN 978-1-4824-2273-3 (pbk.)
 ISBN 978-1-4824-2275-7 (6 pack)
 ISBN 978-1-4824-2274-0 (library binding)
 1. Installations (Art)—Juvenile literature. I. Title.
 N6494.I56W67 2015
 709.04'074—dc23

                          2014035914

First Edition

Published in 2015 by
Gareth Stevens Publishing
111 East 14th Street, Suite 349
New York, NY 10003

© Alix Wood Books

Produced for Gareth Stevens by Alix Wood Books
Designed by Alix Wood
Editor: Eloise Macgregor

Photo credits:
Cover, 11 main, 13 bottom, 14, 17 bottom, 19 top, 20 © Shutterstock; 1, 8 © Mark Jenkins; 4 © Padmayogini/Shutterstock; 5, 28 © Paolo Bona/Shutterstock; 6 © Gerardus; 7 top © Mike Boucher; 7 middle © Gail Leenstra; 7 bottom © Nicholas Smale; 9 top © Jack Two; 9 bottom © Su Justen/Shutterstock; 10 top © Tyburn Mail; 11 top © Arwcheek; 11 bottom © D.A.ST. Arteam; 12 © Chris Howells; 13 top © nga; 15 © Ron Ellis/Shutterstock; 16 top © MoBen; 16 bottom © Comestai; 17 top © Ochkin Alexey/Shutterstock; 18 © Songquan Deng/Shutterstock; 19 bottom © Mpearl; 21 © The Lud; 22 © Jason Brown; 23 top © Dan Sellers; 23 bottom © Isaac Cordal; 24 © Niels; 25 © www.tomassaraceno.com; 26 © Redballproject; 27 © Lewis Tse Pui Lung/Shutterstock; 29 © Richard Cavalleri/Shutterstock

Printed in the United States of America
CPSIA compliance information: Batch # CW15GS: For further information contact Gareth Stevens, New York, New York at 1-800-542-2595.

Contents

What Are Art Installations?

Art installations are **three-dimensional** works of art. Many are designed specially for the place where they are exhibited. Installations can be indoor or outdoor. Sometimes people call outdoor installations "land art." You can usually explore installations by walking in and around them.

Installations give a more **sensory** experience than simply looking at a painting on a wall, or a statue on a pedestal. Some may use new media, such as video or **virtual reality**. Others use traditional art forms such as sculpture.

Arty Fact

Cildo Meireles's installation *Volatile* uses smell, sight, and touch. Visitors walk into a room filled with ash. A candle is at the far end. There is a smell of gas. The sense of danger makes the senses more alert, so the experience is more intense.

This installation by Anish Kapoor is called *Turning the World Upside-Down*. People become part of the installation by being reflected in its mirror-like surface!

This art installation at a design fair is fun to explore. It looks like a colorful town on a hillside. Benches are provided around the exhibit to allow people to sit and look at the installation, too.

There are many different definitions of what people think art is. Which of these do you agree with?

Art is:

- anything that an artist calls art

- something that is created with imagination and skill. It must be either beautiful, or express important ideas or feelings

- a mixture of "form" (the way something is created) and "content" (the "what" that has been created)

WHAT DO YOU THINK?

What do you think makes something an art installation? Does it have to do with the space that the art is displayed in? Or is it more about how much a visitor can interact with the art? Or is it both?

Installation artist Ilya Kabakov said the main actor in an installation, the main focus for which everything is intended, is the viewer.

Art in the Natural World

Many artists like to work with natural materials outdoors. They like the way the artworks change and age over time, just like the landscape around them does.

Outdoor art reaches a large audience. People who would not normally go to galleries can see these artists' work. Land art is made by sculpting the earth into shapes or by making structures using the natural materials found in the landscape.

WHAT DO YOU THINK?

Is it art, or landscaping? Moving piles of earth into a spiral hill may be art. What about creating a deck for your home? Is the hill art because it is original? Or is it because it has no real use?

This spiral hill was created by land artist Robert Smithson.

Andy Goldsworthy is a British sculptor who produces land art for natural and **urban** settings. He uses the natural materials available at the site where the sculpture will be. His materials vary throughout the year. In winter Goldsworthy uses snow, ice, and rocks as his main materials. In autumn he uses leaves, twigs, and trees. If he is by the sea he uses sand, stone, and water.

Goldsworthy's *Storm King Wall* uses local New York stone. It loops around trees and dips down the hillside into a pond, re-emerging on the far shore!

Goldsworthy crafted logs into a pine cone.

Goldsworthy's *Stone House* at a sculpture park in South Yarra, Melbourne, Australia.

Arty Fact

Andy Goldsworthy is also a photographer. If you create land art you need to record your pieces on camera if you want to exhibit them somewhere else. They are difficult to move!

Street Installations

Urban street installations brighten up a city. The difference between street art and a street installation is that street art is done on walls and surfaces, but a street installation uses three-dimensional objects placed in an urban **environment**.

Mark Jenkins is an American artist known for his figures created using sealing tape. He makes them by wrapping tape around himself, sticky side up, and making casts of parts of his body, which he dresses in ordinary clothes. They look very realistic!

Jenkins's installation *Embed*.

Jenkins's installations look so realistic that people have occasionally phoned emergency services when they see one that looks in trouble! Jenkins is interested in the reactions of people to his work, and thinks of them as a social experiment as well as an art project!

Many city streets have been brightened up with uniquely painted sculptures. The identical blank pieces are bought by local organizations and painted in a unique design. The sculptures are then dotted around the city as a public art event, before being sold at auction to raise money for charity.

WHAT DO YOU THINK?

Is it art to just paint a ready-made sculpture that is identical to lots of others? If you think about it, it is no different from painting on an identical-sized canvas as someone else! That's still art. What do you think?

The US Buddy Bear

The 140 United Buddy Bears are an international art exhibition of painted fiberglass bears that hold hands in a circle of peace. Each bear is painted to represent its country.

Blink Or You'll Miss It!

● Some installations only happen for a short period of time. Without a photographic record only the few people who were present at their creation would experience the art. Some installations such as Andy Goldsworthy's outdoor works made of ice or leaves will disappear after a few days.

Many artists like to work in ice. It can be a race against time. Brazilian artist Néle Azevedo creates thousands of small sitting figures from ice, which she has placed on the steps of urban public monuments all over the world. The installations draw attention to climate change, or the loss of life through war.

Néle Azevedo's ice men

Andy Goldsworthy believes that his work grows and then decays as part of a cycle. The photographs he takes show it at the point when he believes the work is most alive.

Some installations can be over in seconds! Chinese artist Cai Guo-Qiang creates explosive installations. This work in Doha, Qatar used military shells and colored smoke. The waiting audience gets a brief sight of the art before it is blown away by the wind!

Triangle by Cai Guo-Qiang.

Arty Fact

The D.A.S.T. Arteam created the enormous sand installation *The Desert Breath*. 89 cones of sand and 89 cone-shaped holes spiral out from a central water-filled pit. The water has since evaporated. Its disintegration is meant to show the passage of time.

View it on a satellite map at coordinates: 27°22'54.59"N, 33°37'48.46"E

WHAT DO YOU THINK?

Why do you think some artists like to work in a material that doesn't last? Is it because of the challenge? Perhaps the fact the sculpture is gradually destroyed adds to its meaning?

Try making your own sand installation and let it be washed away by the tide or rain.

Sculpture or Installation?

What is the difference between a sculpture and an installation? An installation focuses on the space and environment the work is set in. A sculpture focuses on the **subject** of the sculpture itself. Sculptures are not made specifically for one site.

The Antony Gormley piece, *Another Place*, below, is an installation. Cast iron human figures are positioned around a beach, staring out to sea. The arrangement and **scale** of the art creates the impact. The human figures were cast as replicas of Gormley's own body and do not have distinct features. They are meant to be viewed as part of a whole, and not viewed individually as a statue would be.

Gormley wanted the fall of the land, the state of the tide, the weather conditions, and the time of day all to affect the work. At high tide, the sculptures stand up to their necks in water!

This sculpture, *Seated Youth* by Wilhelm Lehmbruck, is also a simple male figure. It is quite different from Gormley's installation, however. The **location** of the sculpture is not important to the work. It could be exhibited anywhere and it would not alter the work. The viewer is meant to focus on the sculpture itself. The viewer can walk around it, but they cannot interact with it like you can with an art installation.

This work, *Seated Youth*, is a statue, not an installation.

Sculptures are designed to be viewed from the outside. Installations surround the viewer in the space of the work.

WHAT DO YOU THINK?

The Fork is a work by Jean-Pierre Zaugg. It is located in Lake Geneva, near Vevey, Switzerland. Do you think *The Fork* is a sculpture or an installation? Do you think a giant fork in a lake is art?

13

Special Events

Festivals and special commemorations sometimes use large, eye-catching art installations to help make them memorable. There is something very magical when an art installation changes a landscape or urban space.

Because many art installations are designed to be temporary, they suit being used at festivals and special events. Do you think it adds value to a piece of art if you can only see it for a limited period of time? Perhaps it makes viewers feel special that they were at the right place at the right time?

This umbrella art installation was designed by Studio Ivotavares for an art festival in Agueda, Portugal. The umbrellas are suspended on thin wires so they appear to float magically in the air!

This installation of ceramic poppies at the Tower of London, UK was created by ceramic artist Paul Cummins and theater stage designer Tom Piper. *Blood Swept Lands and Seas of Red* commemorates 100 years since Britain's involvement in World War I. The 888,246 poppies look spectacular. Each poppy represents someone who was killed during World War I. The poppies will be sold to raise money for military charities.

Arty Fact

The Fallen was designed by Jamie Wardley and Andy Moss as a tribute to those who died on the Normandy beaches during World War II. Using a stencil and a rake, 9000 silhouettes were created on the sand. The figures were washed away by the tide at the end of the day.

WHAT DO YOU THINK?

Would one ceramic poppy be an installation? Or is that simply a ceramic flower? What about 12 poppies? How many poppies do you think you need for a work to become an installation?

Video Installations

Installations usually immerse the viewer in the artist's world. Using video and other **multimedia** is an excellent way to achieve this. Virtual reality can allow the viewer to feel as if they are actually living in a world designed by the artist.

Maurice Benayoun's *Cosmopolis* (above) is created by visitors. Binoculars around the circle show choices of views from 12 different cities. The visitors' choices of video are then projected onto the large screens, to be seen by the people inside the circle.

Maurice Benayoun's giant virtual reality **interactive** installation *Cosmopolis*.

Visitors walk among an installation at Yota Space, an international digital and interactive art festival held in St. Petersburg, Russia.

A changing video installation at the Circle of Light festival in Moscow, Russia.

Maurice Doherty's installation *Eternal Rotation* has two video screens hung back to back in a room. On one screen, there is a front view of a washing machine. Balancing on its top right corner is a goldfish in a bowl. The bowl shakes as the machine washes its load. The other screen shows the same scene, but from above. Because of the positioning of the screens you can't watch both at once. The viewer has to choose one view, otherwise they may miss the bowl falling as they switch sides! The video is surprisingly tense!

WHAT DO YOU THINK?

When does a goldfish bowl on a washing machine become art? Is it when someone puts it in an art gallery? Or is it only art when someone films it and displays it? Is it ever really art?

Public Art

Public art is any type of art that has been designed for a public space. It is designed for people to explore, just like an installation is. Sometimes the art's location is very important, but some public art can move location without taking any value away from it.

Anish Kapoor's *Cloud Gate* is a piece of public art at Millennium Park, Chicago. Visitors are able to walk around and under its high arch. Its surface is like a fun-house mirror distorting people's reflections! Under the arch there is a large dimple. The mirrored surface reflects people standing underneath several times around the dimple!

Anish Kapoor's *Cloud Gate* in Chicago reflects the skyline and the people that walk by. Where it is positioned affects what you see in its mirrored surface.

Dennis Oppenheim's upside down church, *Device to Root Out Evil* was meant to be a temporary installation. It was designed for New York City. They rejected the idea. The work was installed in a park in Vancouver, Canada and then moved to Calgary, Canada. The piece doesn't lose meaning being in another location. A steeple usually points toward the heavens, but this one is pointing toward the earth. What do you think it means?

Oppenheim's *Device to Root Out Evil*.

Arty Fact

Not all public art is popular. Christo and Jeanne-Claude created a $21 million work *The Gates* in Central Park, New York. The exhibit lasted just 16 days! Many people thought it was a waste of money.

The Gates

WHAT DO YOU THINK?

Public art is funded by public money. A city will ask several artists to create ideas for a piece. Then a committee chooses the best idea. So the chosen idea must be art, right?

Comedian Ricky Gervais described *The Gates* as looking like giant Buddhist laundry!

19

Interactive Installations

Interactive installations encourage the spectator to become part of the artwork. Visitors are invited to physically explore and play with the installations. Some work uses modern technology to achieve this, such as motion sensors that trigger something to happen.

American Robert Morris's exhibit *Bodyspacemotionthings* was one of the first interactive pieces, when it was originally shown at the Tate Gallery, London in 1971. People got so involved that 23 visitors needed first aid! It was closed after just four days.

WHAT DO YOU THINK?

When does a playground become art? Do you think Morris's work is beautiful? Does it express important ideas or feelings? Is it art or just fun?

A boy pushes a giant ball around Morris's installation *Bodyspacemotionthings* at the Tate Modern, London in 2009.

Belgian artist Carsten Höller created *Test Site*, a practical art installation for the Tate Modern, London. The slides transport people around the gallery! Visitors can try different shaped slides, and sliders and people watching can all join in the experience.

Arty Fact

Carsten Höller was a scientist before he became an artist. His works sometimes look a little like laboratory equipment, and the public become his experiments!

Test Site by Carsten Höller. Höller described his installation as a sculpture you can travel inside!

Höller enjoys the fun of watching people sliding and knowing the feeling of delight and anxiety experienced by the sliders.

Unusual Spaces

The space where art is displayed is very important for art installations. Artists have picked some very unusual locations! You can find art in a working taxi cab, or even in a small puddle.

The Cab Gallery exterior, *Sunny* by Alex Katz.

Cab Gallery was the idea of art dealer Paul Stolper and art collector and cab driver Jason Brown. Art was exhibited on and in a working London taxi. Artists were given the measurements of the available space usually used by advertisers. Pieces were sent for approval so they would not offend passengers. When the taxi was parked and not for hire, the art could be more ambitious and included work such as sound pieces!

Donald Smith's *Drive-By Random Inner-City Material Colour Space Phenomenon* was placed on the back shelf of the cab!

WHAT DO YOU THINK?

Do you think that art should just be in a gallery, or is it good to find it in unusual places too? Do you think discovering art in an unexpected place makes the experience better?

POLICE TELEPHONE BOX

Artist Isaac Cordal creates tiny sculptures. One of his series of installations features men in suits with briefcases. He places them in the street in gutters, on telephone poles, and in bus shelters. He often puts them in puddles, too! Looking at his work makes you try and imagine a story behind what the figures are doing.

A police box

One of Cordal's tiny installations in a puddle!

Gallery installations

Creating their work for a gallery space can give an artist more control of the environment than they might have outdoors. Artists can create whole worlds for people to explore. Do you think these installations are art, or are they just playgrounds for grown-ups?

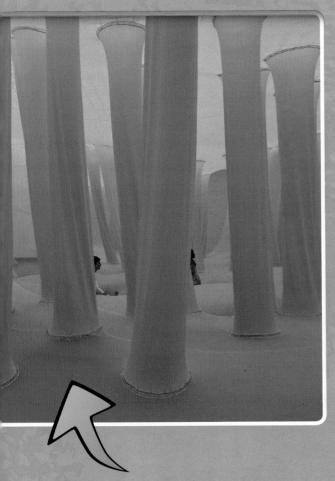

Brazilian artist Ernesto Neto creates large, soft installations that fill an exhibition space. Viewers can walk on or through the installations. The shapes are made of stretchy material stuffed with foam pellets or **aromatic** spices! He sometimes tents the area in fabric to create a room within a room.

Arty Fact

Random International created the installation *The Rain Room* at The Barbican, London. 3D cameras sense your location in the room and automatically turn off water valves above your head. This allows you to walk through a room which is gushing torrential rain without getting wet!

Neto's *Célula Nave* is a giant tented installation created for a gallery in Rotterdam, Netherlands. It is suspended above the ground supported on 18 legs.

Tomás Saraceno's *In Orbit*

To research how to construct his *In Orbit* installation, Tomás Saraceno studied how spiders made their webs!

Suspended above the K21 gallery in Düsseldorf, Germany is Tomás Saraceno's gigantic installation *In Orbit*. The surreal landscape is made using a steel wire mesh. Giant inflated spheres are dotted around the landscape. Visitors can move about in the installation on all three levels. People exploring the work get a great view of other gallery visitors far below them! From below, visitors exploring the work appear as if they are floating!

WHAT DO YOU THINK?

If these installations are art, is a playground art too? How are these installations different from a kids' indoor soft play area? Are they art because they are in a gallery?

Red Balls and Giant Ducks

Some installation artists like to do things on a large scale. And they like to have fun! Kurt Perschke's Red Ball Project and Florentijn Hofman's giant rubber duck have been bringing a smile to people's faces all around the world.

The Red Ball Project is a traveling public art project that places a 15-foot (4.6 m) inflatable red ball in unexpected locations. The ball is inflated in place so that it is wedged in position.

The red ball in Los Angeles, and Paris, France.

People often approach Kurt Perschke with suggestions about where to put the giant red ball in their city. At that moment Perschke believes the people are not spectators but participants in the installation!

Florentijn Hofman wanted to entertain the world with his tour of his giant yellow rubber duck, entitled *Spreading joy around the world*! He wanted to bring back happy childhood memories by exhibiting the duck in 14 cities, starting in his home city, Amsterdam, Netherlands.

Arty Fact

Hofman built various sizes of rubber duck. The **prototype** was only 1 inch (2.5 cm) tall. The largest rubber duck was 85x66x105 feet (26x20x32 m) and weighed over 1,300 lb (600 kg)!

WHAT DO YOU THINK?

The sheer size of these installations, and their humor, creates a talking point wherever they go. Hofman believes his duck can relieve the world's tensions. Do you think that if art brings a smile to people's faces it is more valuable than art that doesn't?

The duck floating in Hong Kong's Victoria Harbor.

Are Installations Art?

Have you made up your mind? Are art installations art? To help you, have a look at some of these arguments "for" and "against."

Installations Are Art

- Installations attract people who think they are art
- Galleries consider the pieces to be art, so they must be
- Installations can make an area more interesting
- The artists are expressing themselves
- Installations can attract tourists from around the world
- Installations use recognized art forms such as sculpture, painting, and music

Installations Aren't Art

- If a big yellow duck is art, why isn't a mass-produced rubber duck art too?
- Many installations are just play areas for adults
- Some installations only last for a brief time and are gone. Art needs to be lasting
- Many installations are fun. Shouldn't art be serious?
- You could fill a room with smoke and call it an installation. It's not art, just a room filled with smoke

Jaume Plensa's *Crown Fountain* in Millennium Park, Chicago.

Crown Fountain cost $17 million to create! The Crown family, after whom it is named, donated $10 million. The rest of the money was made up by other private donations. Those people must have thought it was art!

Installation art often relies on the idea of a viewer's presence in the space. This can lead to a problem when you try to decide if it is art or not. If you have not personally experienced it, it is hard to judge whether it worked as a piece of art. A little like a joke that isn't funny when repeated, you really had to have been there.

WHAT DO YOU THINK?

If you are not sure, that's OK. Perhaps some installations could be called art and some couldn't? Which artists or which types of installation do you think could be called art?

Glossary

aromatic
Having a noticeable and usually pleasant smell.

environment
The area surrounding something.

interactive
Involving the actions or input of a user such as an interactive museum exhibit; allowing two-way communications such as between a person and a computer.

location
A place having some particular use, such as an ideal place for a sculpture to be placed.

multimedia
Using or composed of more than one form of communication or expression, such as multimedia software that combines sound, video, and text.

prototype
An original thing on which a thing is modeled.

scale
The size of a picture, plan, or model in comparison to other things.

sensory
Of or relating to sensation or to the senses.

subject
The person or thing discussed or focused on.

surreal
Where elements are combined in a strange way that you would not normally expect, such as in a dream.

three-dimensional
Giving the appearance of depth or varying distances.

urban
Of, relating to, typical of, or being a city.

virtual reality
An artificial environment which is experienced through sights and sounds provided by a computer and in which one's actions partly decide what happens in the environment.

For More Information

Books

Greve, Tom. *A Look at Urban Art*. Vero Beach, FL: Rourke Publishing Group, 2013.

McLean, Linda K. *The Heidelberg Project: A Street of Dreams*. Northville, MI: Nelson Publishing and Marketing, 2007.

Sutherland, Adam. Street Style: *Street Art*. Minneapolis, MN: Lerner, 2012.

Websites

Tiny Rotten Peanuts
http://tinyrottenpeanuts.com/kids-learn-installation-art-christo-and-jeanne-claude/
An introduction to the installation art of Christo and Jeanne-Claude for children.

http://tinyrottenpeanuts.com/kids-learn-installation-art-andy-goldsworthy/
An introduction to installation art of Andy Goldsworthy for children.

Publisher's note to educators and parents:
Our editors have carefully reviewed these websites to ensure that they are suitable for students. Many websites change frequently, however, and we cannot guarantee that a site's future contents will continue to meet our high standards of quality and educational value. Be advised that students should be closely supervised whenever they access the Internet.

Index